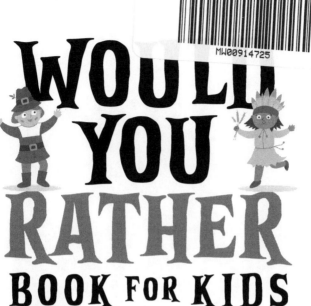

# WOULD YOU RATHER

# BOOK FOR KIDS

THANKSGIVING EDITION

**300+ Fun and Festive Holiday Questions for Kids Ages 7-13**

## This Book Belongs to

_____

_____

## Thanks!

Thank you for your purchase. If you enjoyed this book, please consider dropping us a review. It takes only 5 seconds and helps small independent publishers like ours.

# CONTENTS

# INTRODUCTION

Step into the cozy world of *Would You Rather Book for Kids: Thanksgiving Edition*. This heartwarming and laughter-filled book serves up a cornucopia of Thanksgiving-themed conundrums, prompting children to make choices as delightful as a perfectly roasted turkey. Through whimsical scenarios and cranberry-inspired adventures, it helps kids sharpen their decision-making skills while dishing out extra helpings of Thanksgiving merriment. It's perfect for parties, sleepovers, game nights, vacations, or road trips. Of course, you can even play it by yourself! Whichever you decide, you'll have a fantastically-festive time!

# THANKSGIVING WOULD YOU RATHER
# FAQs

Hey there, Thanksgiving enthusiasts! We've got answers to your burning questions about our awesome game.

## HOW MANY PLAYERS?

You need at least two players, but the more, the merrier! If you have a big group, consider splitting into smaller ones for maximum fun.

## WHO GOES FIRST?

To kick things off, let's get creative! The player born closest to Thanksgiving gets the honor of starting the game.

## HOW TO PLAY?

First, you'll need your questions. Each player takes turns picking a random question from the book. The first player asks it to someone (or everyone), and play continues clockwise. (Don't forget to ask *why* they chose the answer they did.) Keep going until all questions are answered or it's time for more celebrating!

## IS THERE A TIME LIMIT?

It's your call. If you want to speed things up and add some excitement, set a timer. Quick answers can be hilarious, especially for the super-silly questions!

Now go out there and gobble up the good times!

# 1

# THANKSGIVING DINNER DILEMMAS

Would you rather have turkey as the main dish

## or

ham as the main dish on Thanksgiving?

Would you rather cook a big Thanksgiving meal

## or

have it catered?

Would you rather spend Thanksgiving with your extended family

## or

have a quiet dinner with just your immediate family?

THANK

Would you rather eat
pumpkin pie for dessert
on Thanksgiving

## or

apple pie?

Would you rather watch
the Macy's Thanksgiving Day
Parade on TV

## or

in person?

THANK

Would you rather have a traditional Thanksgiving feast

**or**

try a completely new and unique menu?

Would you rather host Thanksgiving at your home

**or**

travel to someone else's home for the holiday?

Would you rather savor the last piece of pumpkin pie

**or**

the final helping of mashed potatoes?

Would you rather have a Thanksgiving without any mashed potatoes

## or

without any stuffing?

Would you rather have a Thanksgiving dinner with no cranberry sauce

## or

no gravy?

Would you rather have Thanksgiving without any pumpkin-flavored dishes

## or

without any sweet potato dishes?

Would you rather have a Thanksgiving feast with all your favorite dishes but eat alone

## or

have a simple meal with loved ones?

Would you rather have all the classic side dishes but no turkey

## or

with turkey but no traditional side dishes?

Would you rather have a Thanksgiving with all homemade dishes

## or

order everything from your favorite restaurant?

## Would you rather have Thanksgiving without any desserts

## or

### without any appetizers?

## Would you rather cook the Thanksgiving meal

## or

### clean up the dishes?

THANK

Would you rather attend a Thanksgiving potluck where everyone brings a dish

## or

a formal sit-down dinner at a fancy restaurant?

Would you rather have a Thanksgiving without any rolls

## or

without any mashed potatoes and gravy?

Would you rather spend the day cooking Thanksgiving dinner

## or

decorating your home for the holiday?

THANK

Would you rather have a
Thanksgiving feast with
unlimited leftovers

## or

just enough for one meal?

Would you rather your home
always smell like turkey

## or

always smell like apple pie?

Would you rather eat an entire
turkey by yourself

## or

eat all the stuffing by yourself?

THANK

Would you eat a burnt-to-a-crisp Thanksgiving dinnerThanksgiving dinner

## or

an undercooked Thanksgiving dinner?

Would you rather eat Thanksgiving dinner with your favorite celebrity

## or

with your own family?

Would you rather always feel too full

## or

always feel a little hungry?

Would you rather drink hot cocoa with your Thanksgiving meal

## or

hot apple cider?

Would you rather the turkey be burned, but have an otherwise perfect meal

## or

burn everything but the turkey, which is cooked perfect?

THANK

Would you rather eat as much as you want of your meal but not be able to taste your food

## or

only be able to eat one bite of each of foof but have it taste perfectly delicious?

Would you rather get 10 dollars for every slice of pie you ate

## or

get 100 dollars for eating no Thanksgiving food at all?

Would you rather stuff yourself with Thanksgiving dinner wearing pants two sizes too small

## or

wear pants two sizes too big and only get one bite of each side?

THANK

Would you rather have a surprise guest for Thanksgiving dinner

## or

surprise someone else by showing up at their door?

Would you rather dine at the White House

## or

at Rockefeller Center for Thanksgiving?

Would you rather have Thanksgiving dinner on a beach in Hawaii

## or

in a cozy log cabin during a snowstorm?

# 2

# THANKSGIVING FOOD ADVENTURES

Would you rather go for a week gobbling like a turkey when you try to speak

## or

only talking (and spitting) with your mouth full?

Would you rather have nice hair that gets in your mouth every time you try to eat

## or

be totally bald?

Would you rather always smell like turkey

## or

always smell like gravy?

THANK

Would you rather wash your
hair with gravy

## or

with cranberry sauce?

Would you rather go school
wearing a hollow pumpkin
on your head

## or

covered in turkey feathers?

Would you rather eat an entire Thanksgiving meal with just your hands

## or

drink an entire Thanksgiving meal after it's been liquified in a blender?

Would you rather be a turkey in a Thanksgiving school play

## or

a corn on the cob?

Would you rather eat cold turkey

## or

melted ice cream?

Would you rather not be allowed to speak on Thanksgiving

## or

not be allowed to have Thanksgiving dessert?

Would you rather have Thanksgiving in the time before electricity

## or

have Thanksgiving on the International Space Station?

Would you rather take an expensive Thanksgiving vacation in Paris

## or

eat an expensive Thanksgiving in your home dinner prepared by a world famous chef?

THANK

Would you rather get the largest serving of stuffing

## or

the largest slice of pie?

Would you rather have your favorite Hollywood celebrity join you for Thanksgiving dinner

## or

your favorite sports star?

Would you rather have the hiccups all Thanksgiving Day

## or

have to fart every five minutes?

THANK

Would you rather have
a constant itch during
Thanksgiving dinner

## or

a runny nose?

Would you rather burp loudly
in front of everyone at the
Thanksgiving dinner table

## or

fart quietly in front of everyone?

Would you rather wear a blindfold and not see your food

## or

wear nose plugs and not smell your food?

Would you rather eat a bowl of raw pumpkin

## or

a bowl of cold gravy?

Would you rather eat mashed potatoes that taste like toothpaste

## or

cranberry sauce that tastes like ketchup?

THANK

Would you rather have gravy on your pumpkin pie

## or

chocolate syrup on your turkey?

Would you rather eat stuffing with chocolate chips

## or

turkey with sprinkles?

Would you rather drink cranberry juice that tastes like gravy

## or

eat turkey that tastes like brussels sprouts?

Would you rather have a plate of brussels sprouts for dessert

## or

a plate of rainbow sprinkles for a meal?

Would you rather eat cranberry sauce that's as spicy as hot sauce

## or

stuffing that's as sweet as candy?

Would you rather only be allowed to eat cranberry sauce for the entire Thanksgiving meal

## or

eat turkey that's incredibly dry?

Would you rather have a Thanksgiving dinner with no forks

## or

a Thanksgiving dinner with no plates?

Would you rather have a pet turkey

## or

a pet pig?

Would you rather eat a burnt
turkey dinner

**or**

burnt desserts?

Would you rather eat green
beans that taste like licorice

**or**

sweet potatoes that taste
like mustard?

Would you rather have pumpkin
pie with ketchup as a topping

**or**

turkey with mayonaise on it?

THANK

Would you rather have gravy
on your pancakes

## or

maple syrup on your turkey?

Would you rather skip
the turkey with gravy

## or

skip dessert during your
Thanksgiving dinner?

Would you rather have
Thanksgiving leftovers every
day for a week

## or

never get to eat them at all?

THANK

Would you rather eat Thanksgiving dinner with chopsticks

**or**

with your hands?

Would you rather wear a turkey costume

**or**

a pilgrim costume to the Thanksgiving table?

Would you rather have a Thanksgiving snowball fight

**or**

a Thanksgiving food fight?

# 3
# THANKSGIVING FUN & GAMES

Would you rather participate in a Thanksgiving parade dressed as a turkey

## or

dressed as a pilgrim?

Would you rather eat your own weight in cranberry sauce

## or

drink your own weight in gravy?

Would you rather express gratitude before every bite

## or

sing a song after each bite during your Thanksgiving meal?

Would you rather spend Thanksgiving in New York City

## or

on a farm in the country?

Would you rather ride on a Thanksgiving parade float

## or

march with a band?

Would you rather have
unlimited turkey

## or

your favorite
Thanksgiving dessert?

Would you rather sit at the
adult table

## or

the kids' table for
Thanksgiving dinner?

Would you rather watch the
Macy's Thanksgiving Day
Parade at home

## or

march in the parade during
a rain storm?

Would you rather take a post-Thanksgiving dinner nap

## or

go outside for some fresh air?

Would you rather attend the original Thanksgiving

## or

a Thanksgiving celebration in the year 2050?

Would you rather have cold turkey for Thanksgiving

## or

cold gravy?

THANK

Would you rather be a part of the Macy's Thanksgiving Day Parade

## or

be a guest on a Thanksgiving cooking show?

Would you rather help prepare a Thanksgiving feast for your local community

## or

donate toys to children in need?

Would you rather establish a new Thanksgiving family tradition

## or

receive a surprise gift each year?

Would you rather dine in
your pajamas

## or

in formal attire for
Thanksgiving dinner?

Would you rather don
a pilgrim hat

## or

a feather headdress for
Thanksgiving?

Would you rather play a game of charades after dinner

## or

go for a brisk walk?

Would you rather have a Thanksgiving feast with a choice of delicious vegan meal options

## or

a choice of delicious vegan dessert options?

Would you rather embark on a Thanksgiving-themed treasure hunt after dinner

## or

partake in a festive crafting session?

Would you rather have your
Thanksgiving meal at home

## or

at Disney World?

Would you rather decorate
your house with autumn colors
for Thanksgiving

## or

adorn it with twinkling
Christmas lights?

Would you rather lead the
Thanksgiving parade as a turkey

## or

end the parade as Santa Claus?

THANK

Would you rather peel
50 potatoes

## or

slice 10 onions?

Would you rather enjoy a
peaceful Thanksgiving meal
with just your immediate family

## or

a lively, fun-filled dinner with
all your relatives and friends?

Would you rather have a
Thanksgiving picnic in a park

## or

a formal dinner at home?

Would you rather take a horse-drawn sleigh ride after dinner

## or

go on a family hike?

Would you rather perform a Thanksgiving comedy skit with your family

## or

write and perform a silly Thanksgiving song?

THANK

Would you rather have your Thanksgiving dinner on a plane

**or**

your dinner on a train?

Would you rather have the ability to cook Thanksgiving dinner with a snap of your fingers

**or**

instantly clean up after dinner with a snap of your fingers?

Would you rather spend Thanksgiving Day volunteering at a soup kitchen

**or**

visiting lonely senior citizens?

Would you rather attend an NFL football game

## or

the Macy's Thanksgiving Day Parade?

Would you rather have a magical oven that cooks everything perfectly

## or

a magical dishwasher that cleans up instantly?

Would you rather engage in a friendly game of charades

## or

test your wits with a Thanksgiving-themed trivia quiz?

Would you rather create handmade Thanksgiving decorations

**or**

design a Thanksgiving-themed centerpiece?

Would you rather engage in a friendly game of touch football

**or**

have a family talent show after dinner?

Would you rather play football with your family

**or**

watch football on TV after dinner?

Would you rather participate in a turkey trot run on Thanksgiving morning

## or

sleep in?

Would you rather cook and clean up Thanksgiving dinner

## or

shop for everyone in your family on Black Friday?

Would you rather volunteer
at a local charity on
Thanksgiving Day

## or

have a quiet day at home?

Would you rather have a
Thanksgiving with perfect
weather for an outdoor meal

## or

cozy up indoors on a rainy
or snowy day?

Would you rather spend
Thanksgiving weekend shopping
for Black Friday deals

## or

relaxing at home?

Would you rather share what you're thankful for before

## or

after the Thanksgiving meal?

Would you rather take a bath in cranberry sauce

## or

go swimming in a pool of apple cider?

Would you rather be a balloon handler in the Macy's Thanksgiving Day Parade

## or

a float rider?

THANK

Would you rather watch the parade from a cozy, heated indoor spot

## or

brave the cold on the streetside for the best view?

Would you rather have a front-row seat to the parade

## or

a behind-the-scenes tour of how it's organized?

Would you rather have a balloon in the shape of your favorite cartoon character

## or

one representing your favorite Thanksgiving dish?

Would you rather march with a band playing your favorite instrument in the parade

## or

be a part of a dance troupe?

Would you rather dress up as a historical figure for a Thanksgiving parade

## or

as a character from your favorite book or movie?

THANK

Would you rather wear a colorful costume and perform a dance routine during the parade

## or

narrate the parade on live TV?

Would you rather ride in a horse-drawn carriage through the parade

## or

be chauffeured in a classic convertible?

Would you rather participate in a community Thanksgiving parade

## or

attend the famous Macy's Thanksgiving Day Parade in New York City?

Would you rather be responsible for inflating and deflating the parade balloons

## or

managing the sound and music on a float?

Would you rather design your own parade float from scratch

## or

help decorate an existing one with your creative ideas?

Would you rather attend a parade with traditional marching bands

## or

one featuring futuristic, high-tech performances?

THANK

Would you rather be a clown entertaining the crowd

**or**

the parade's grand marshal, leading the way?

Would you rather watch a parade with intricate, detailed floats

**or**

a parade featuring giant, eye-catching balloons?

Would you rather have a parade-themed party with friends at home

**or**

attend a live parade event in your city?

Would you rather be in charge of the fireworks finale at the end of a parade

## or

the confetti cannons during the procession?

Would you rather be the official parade timekeeper, ensuring everything stays on schedule

## or

the parade announcer, describing the floats and performers to the audience?

Would you rather have a parade with a "Winter Wonderland" theme

## or

a "Fantasy Adventure" theme?

THANK

Made in the USA
Middletown, DE
19 November 2024

64989819R00035